CW01626869

How to E
Emerging Adults in Church

Rebecca Glover
Digital Communications Coordinator at Youth for Christ

GROVE BOOKS LIMITED
RIDLEY HALL RD CAMBRIDGE CB3 9HU

Contents

Acknowledgments

Thank you to Nigel Roberts, who supported me in the writing of this Grove booklet from when it started as my dissertation. Thanks also to Youth for Christ, everyone who shared their stories with me, and church leaders who invested in me as an emerging adult

The cover image is copyright © Grove Books Ltd

Copyright © Rebecca Glover 2022

First Impression September 2022
ISSN 1748-3492
ISBN 978 1 78827 265 0

1 Introduction

> 'Today's key challenge for the church in the West is to reach and raise the next generations—often missing and misunderstood—yet vital to the future of contemporary society and to Christianity.'
>
> Nick Allan and Marjorie Allan[1]

Picture This

You are nineteen years old, too old for the youth group now. You have spent the last few years leaving the main church service part way through to join other young people in a programme aimed specifically at those in your age stage. You have learnt key biblical stories and practical life lessons through role play, reading, discussion, activities and games. However, now you are an adult, so you are in the main church service with the rest of the adults. The preacher today is providing practical application for the Scripture, but they keep mentioning jobs and family. You are a student, you are not sure what you want to do long term, and you do not have a spouse or children. In fact, your parents and siblings are over one hundred miles away, back in your home town. Throughout the sermon, there have been a couple of references to popular culture…in the eighties, so they have gone right over your head. The sermon is 50 minutes long, so you sit and listen, trying to take notes. But you miss the games and the discussions, even if you were beginning to feel too old for it.

Eventually you stand to sing the final song and you enjoy the lyrics; perhaps you recognize one of the choruses from a psalm you read. But these songs do not sound much like the music you listen to outside of church, and you are not sure what some of the lyrics really mean. You make a mental note to Google what 'cherubim and seraphim' means later on.

Everyone gets up to mingle with their coffees and teas in hand, but you feel out of place. There are not many people your age or at your stage; not like when you were in youth group.

This was my experience of church as an emerging adult. Too old for youth group, but too young to really feel part of adult church. Therefore, although

I am writing this still as an emerging adult, I wanted to get involved in the conversation: how do we successfully engage emerging adults in church?

What This Is, and What This Is Not

This booklet is not a tool to bash emerging adults or church leaders with. I do not suggest that all emerging adults have a similar experience to my own, or that this is an international problem in which no churches are succeeding, and you hold the answers in your hands. I believe in the power of intergenerational church, and so I will not be boxing people in, or suggesting that leaders plant an Emerging Adults Only Church. This booklet is, however, a collection of stories and research, a reflective piece that asks you questions, and a stepping stone into engaging emerging adults in church. Finally, whilst this booklet is aimed at the more traditional idea of church (described as 'a building for Christian religious activities' by the *Cambridge Dictionary*), let us have a broad idea of ecclesiology. The first church was a group of people who, after hearing Paul's teaching of Jesus, repented, were baptized and received the Spirit. They devoted themselves to teachings and fellowship, they broke bread together in their homes, and every day they met in the temple courts (Acts 2.38–46). For the 'New Testament, the church is a distinctive way of life, defined by common practices, centred in a relationship to the Lordship of Jesus.'[2] So, let us engage emerging adults in church, whatever church looks like for your context.

Who Are Emerging Adults?

Every generation is labelled with general characteristics based on social and cultural factors. However, labelling generations can lead to finger-pointing and prejudice; it can create older generations as perpetrators and younger generations as victims. Generational labels simplify human intricacies and complexities. Sure, these labels can be useful for learning about each other. Youth for Christ has produced much research on Gen Z and, born in 1999, I find myself relating to the findings. Yes, family and friends have the highest influence on me. Yes, I spend most of my spare time online.[3] This research can be beneficial in directing how we evangelize, disciple and 'do' mission. However, for a BBC Bitesize article to suggest that millennials are obsessed with avocados feels much like a Buzzfeed quiz telling me whether or not I have yet met my soulmate, based on my favourite childhood film.[4] It does not make sense.

I also feel that, in this instance, it could be limiting and time-bounding. Therefore, I am using the term 'emerging adulthood,' which recognizes the unique characteristics of this new and particular phase of life. Like other generational labels, the age brackets of this term are widely argued. Some say that emerging adults are those aged between eighteen and twenty-five. Others say that this middle ground does not exist, it is just an extension of adolescence, whilst others stretch the term to eighteen to thirty. I feel that is too big a stretch, as those aged eighteen are often in a completely different stage of their life to those in their thirties. So, from here on out, read 'emerging adults' as around eighteen- to twenty-five-year-olds.

It All Starts With a Vision

> I keep asking that the God of our Lord Jesus Christ, the glorious Father, may give you the Spirit of wisdom and revelation, so that you may know him better. I pray that the eyes of your heart may be enlightened in order that you may know the hope to which he has called you, the riches of his glorious inheritance in his holy people, and his incomparably great power for us who believe.
>
> Eph 1.17–19 (NIV)

Like anything within the church, it is hard to commence something that is sustainable and fruitful without vision. Sometimes, emerging adult ministries are not prioritized because there is not a vision, the age group is not seen as important, or it simply is not considered. Or perhaps there is not money in the budget to hire an emerging adults leader, and other staff and volunteers are overburdened already. Instead of praying for wisdom and revelation, and for eyes to be opened for new ways, we press the stop button. I believe that with God's wisdom and vision, the church can successfully engage emerging adults. Not so that the church can give itself a tap on the back and be awarded the 'multigenerational' badge. But for the growth of the kingdom, and so that emerging adults too can have a relationship with their first love, Jesus.

Reflection

- Read the verses above again, write them down, and spend a couple of minutes reflecting on them.
- What words, phrases, or ideas stand out to you?
- What has emerging adult ministry looked like in your church context in the past?
- Pray that God would give you a fresh vision, wisdom, discernment, and would open the eyes of your heart to emerging adult ministry.
- What do you feel God might be saying? You may like to draw or write it out.

2 The Facts and Figures

In 2020, YouGov shared research that said '41% of Britons believe there is neither "a god" nor "a higher power." Younger generations are the most likely to think there is no greater force out there.'[5]

In 2022, the 'Talking Jesus Report' showed that 48% of the 4000 people surveyed described themselves as Christian. Just 29% of these were 19–24, which was the smallest age group. 26% of the respondents did not affiliate with any of the main religions.

The age group 18–24 has the highest percentage of those choosing 'none,' at 27%.[6]

The Evangelical Alliance says, 'The church in the UK is missing a generation of young adults from our congregations' and in 2018, employed a Head of Missions to Young Adults for the first time.[7]

2013 research, 'Authentic Faith: Fresh Expressions of Church Amongst Young Adults,' said that only 11% of regular churchgoers are between the ages of 25 and 34, whilst 16% of the UK population is within that age group.[8]

Meanwhile in the US, The Barna Group discovered that 59% of eighteen- to twenty-nine-year-olds have dropped out of American churches after attending regularly.[9]

31% of 18–29 year olds surveyed in America described the church as boring, 24% said it is not relevant, whilst 23% said church does not prepare them for real life. Two-thirds of American millennials believe churchgoers to be hypocritical (this is actually echoed in the 'Talking Jesus Report,' but not in this age range). Emerging adults also have experienced the church as doubtless, over-protective, shallow and anti-science.

Despite being research from across the pond, I think emerging adults in the UK can relate somewhat.

What Can These Facts and Figures Tell Us?

A small number of young adults in Britain would identify as Christians. Therefore, when doing freshers' events or promoting posts on social media, it is likely that you will not be inviting believers to church but atheists, agnostics or those of other faiths. Your mission goes from 'just' inviting Christian freshers to your church after they have moved away from their own, but you are also perhaps evangelizing. The following chapters explore attractional models, creating community, authenticity and being intentional; all are important things when inviting both believers and non-believers to church.

There is much more research from America than from the UK about why emerging adults are not in church, and how to engage the ones that are. This fact in itself suggests that perhaps we are just not prioritizing engaging emerging adults.

Emerging adults in America have experience of and see the church as doubtless, overprotective, shallow and anti-science. Could you find out how emerging adults in your area feel about the church, and are there ways you can begin to reverse that? For example, if emerging adults feel that the church is anti-science, could you hold a TED Talk-style evening with a Christian scientist? Or could you hold a 'roast a Christian' evening, where emerging adults have an opportunity to ask their leaders questions about their faith and about the Bible? With leaders' vulnerability of perhaps exploring some of these big questions themselves, emerging adults may begin to see the church as authentic, and a place to explore doubts and big questions.

Jacob's Story

When I was eighteen, I joined a new church after moving away from my home city for university. There were people at the door ready to welcome me with a handshake, and when I was through the doors I was met with smiles. I wandered into the hall slowly, taking everything in, and sat on my own. I noticed another couple of young adults, but quickly also noticed the baby they had in their arms, and the toddler at their feet.

There were no smoke machines or LED coloured lights, which I liked. Nothing flashy, it felt real. I liked the few songs we sang, but I never quite connected with the sermons. It had lots of Bible study, explained who the different characters were, and I agreed with the church's theology—it wasn't that. But I just couldn't see how it was relevant to me. I didn't really see how it was relevant to the older generations sitting around me either, to be honest. It was all head knowledge, like it was most important to know what happens in the Bible, like we're at a book club or something. I longed to relate to something, to someone. I wanted to know how to share my faith in my university, how to set healthy and godly boundaries, I wanted to know how to pray.

The minister spoke to me after the service and asked about where I'm from, my family, and what I'm studying at university, and I had similar conversations with others too. But, just as during the service, I longed to relate. Everyone I spoke to had busy jobs, and children, and many hadn't heard of the subject I was studying at university. It was nice that they asked questions though.

I noticed a news board on the wall, that had leaflets about debt charities and food bank, a who's who poster, and a list of groups and activities that happen during the week: baby group, toddler group, youth group, men's breakfast, a board game group for the retired, and a women's choir. No space for me.

On the fifth week, another young adult attended. He said that he was just home for the weekend, and this was his family church growing up. I mentioned that there aren't many young adults here, and asked whether they've all gone to uni now, like himself. He replied, 'There never has been many young adults here. I think they mostly go to the church round the corner. They have a really great worship band, and they meet for pizza and this thing called "Life Chats," where they read the Bible and talk about how it fits with their life. Or there's another one, on the other side of town. You might have seen them at freshers' fayre—they usually give out bags of like instant noodles, vouchers, and leaflets about their services.'

On the sixth week, I walked in alone again. I sat on my own again. I listened to a 45-minute talk about what Moses used to build the tabernacle. I stood on my own, until a man who had already spoken to me two weeks ago asked, 'Are you new here?' And then I left, alone.

On the seventh week, I went to one of the student churches instead.

Attraction

3

Is it Okay?

The argument about whether attractional models of church are okay has been tossing back and forth for years. You may have heard people say they have left church because they 'didn't get anything from it', perhaps they weren't *enjoying* the worship. There is a stereotype, I think, that particularly emerging adults are wrongly attracted to the big, bright megachurches; worship teams not dissimilar to gigs with lights and smoke machines, held in a warehouse. There are arguments to say that attractive churches are not authentic, give in to consumer culture, and are a sign of spiritual immaturity. Others argue that it is no different to simply having preferences and different learning styles, and attractional models are invitational for non-Christians.[10] Furthermore, there is an argument that whilst the debate is useful for us to explore more effective approaches and ideas for expanding God's kingdom, does it really matter if the lost are 'entering the kingdom of heaven through the front door of an attractional church or the side door of a Starbucks.'[11]

I think this is a huge conversation for another time, and from my research, experience and other literature, it is clear that being attracted to various elements of church is vital for emerging adults to be first engaged. However, that attraction then needs to be backed up with and lead to Jesus-centred discipleship.

Church can be viewed as attractive when it is relevant, authentic and with particular teaching and sung worship, which we will explore in this chapter.

Relevance

Among emerging adults, there is a need for tailor-made, relevant teaching that discusses age stage issues, professional development, big questions, discipleship, finances, relationships, sexuality and identity, whether in a Sunday service preach, or in midweek small groups. This links back to Kinnaman's US research, that found that emerging adults feel church is doubtless, anti-science and irrelevant. These points can be reversed in the right spaces.

Again, just with any age group, emerging adults want to hear teaching that has relevant application. Emerging adults want to know what the Bible has to do with them today.

Have you ever sat through a sermon, been in a work meeting, or have had the radio on whilst driving, and have zoned out, but once you hear a reference to a show you are watching, a popular current news item or a story, you snap back in again? Having regular and relevant stories, clips and references can keep emerging adults engaged.

Authenticity

Emerging adults and young people are generations acutely aware of inauthenticity. Articles and documentaries telling of scandals both inside and outside of the church are at their fingertips, 'most watched' on Netflix and 'trending' on Twitter. Emerging adults are attracted to authentic church. Churches that do not just preach from the lectern about how we should walk humbly, act justly, love mercy, but practice this by being on the streets at soup kitchens, offering their building for counselling charities to use, and are environmentally conscious. Emerging adults want to see faith in action.

A Student and Young Adults curate I spoke to said that relationship has been formed and she has seen fruit from her being vulnerable and opening up first. Emerging adults see that she has not got it all together, that she does not know all the answers and is too navigating the messiness of life, and they see authenticity.

Beth Keith's report on authentic faith said that church is about journeying and working out life together in the messiness. Honesty and not being detached from faith is integral to leadership.[1212] Again, this authenticity is attractive to emerging adults.

Sung Worship and Teaching

Worship and teaching are significant aspects of our church experience; they are perhaps the two elements that take up the most time in a service, perhaps the two elements of church that can be expected to feature in an order of service week in, week out. Therefore, it is no wonder that this is a subtheme of an emerging adult's attraction to a church.

Emerging adults that I spoke to shared with me their reflection that church is so different from every other context they find themselves in. The music does not sound the same to what they listen to outside church, and although they sit in classes and lectures where they may be talked at for hours at a time, the teaching includes different learning styles, classes include discussion times and activities. The likes of TikTok are potentially affecting young people and emerging adults' attention span, as they scroll through an endless feed of videos that last no more than a couple of minutes. Many adults do not have the attention span to listen to a long sermon—how can we expect emerging adults to do the same?

A church leader I spoke to said that it was not about a complete overhaul, but 'itching where emerging adults are scratching, whilst reaching older generations too.' They said that their services often include a mixture of hymns and modern music, recognizing the power of both genres, the potentional to meet with Jesus of both, but also recognizing the needs and wants of different generations.

Case Study

Denomination: Anglican

Geography: Midlands, university city

Emerging adults: Approximately 60

Context: 6pm service specifically aimed at students and emerging adults.

Pre-service: a promotional Instagram post is uploaded in the days before the service, which gives details of the timings, location and sermon title.

The leaders upload another Instagram post of them setting up for the service, with a reminder of the time, location, sermon title and the pre-service snack available.

Pre-service: doughnuts, tea and coffee are available at the back of church whilst the congregation arrives. It is a traditional Anglican building, decorated with small plant pots on windowsills and fairy lights strung around pillars.

At 6pm, music plays loudly through the speakers and a timer counts down on screen. The congregation sit on the chairs towards the front of the church.

Introduction: the leader welcomes everyone, introduces themselves, and asks that the congregation turn towards each other to share a highlight of their week. After a couple of minutes, the leader regathers everyone and invites people to share with the group.

Game: the leader introduces the tray game and asks for two volunteers. At the front is a tray with various items on: a peg, car keys, a banana, a pencil, lip balm, a Bible, a battery, a soft toy, a phone charger. The two volunteers have two minutes to look at the contents of the tray, before it is covered with a tea towel. The pair then take it in turns to try and list every item on the tray. The rest of the congregation is encouraged to cheer along. A photo is taken, that will be uploaded to their social media account, so that followers have a visual idea of what happens at an evening service.

Worship song: Move Your Heart, Maverick City

Worship song: All Hail King Jesus, Bethel Music

Worship song: Here I Am to Worship, Hillsong

Talk: Knowing God. A new teaching series about connecting with God. To know we are loved, seen and known by him, but what does this mean in reality?

Response: the congregation are invited to go to the front, where someone on the prayer team will pray with them.

Worship song: Build My Life, Housefires

Post service: the congregation help to set chairs up for a group the following morning, before many of the students and young adults go to the local pub.

Case Study

Denomination: Assemblies of God

Geography: South East England town

Emerging adults: Approximately two

Context: Post-Sunday morning family service

The family service included:

Worship song: Our God is a Great Big God, Vineyard Kids

Worship song: Be Thou My Vision, Stuart Townend

All-age slot: an Olympic-themed quiz. Two sides of the church were split to compete against each other.

Reading: John 21

Sermon: Last Moments—a teaching series that looked at Jesus appearing to the disciples before ascending to heaven.

Worship song: When I Survey, Kathryn Scott

Worship song: Happy Day, Tim Hughes

After the service, the volunteer student worker invited the two regular emerging adults, as well as a new student, to the local pub for lunch. They discussed the highs and lows of their week, their reflections on the talk and what topics they would like to see the church speak on this term.

The student worker gifted the new student a new student box, which included a list of local supermarkets, dentists, GP surgeries, and contact details for the church, as well as a bag of sweets, a water bottle and a pack of pens with church branding, and a book of the psalms. The student worker did not know the new student would be attending this week, but they kept a stack of new student boxes in their office.

Finally, the group spoke about an emerging adult weekend event that was upcoming and planned to book tickets and organize transport. The emerging adults considered whether they have any friends they could also bring along.

Case Study

Denomination: Pentecostal

Geography: North East England

Emerging Adults: Approximately 120

Context: Midweek barbeque and worship. This was a social event in replacement of weekly connect groups.

Pre-event: promotional Instagram posts were uploaded in the weeks before the event, which gave details of the timings and location. Emerging adults were asked to sign up through an online form.

Emerging adults began to arrive at 7pm. There was space in the foyer and outside in the courtyard. This time was unstructured; leaders were preparing the barbeque, stewarding the car park, and some were going between groups to catch up with the emerging adults.

Music played in the background. A PlayStation and a photo booth were also available.

By 7.30pm, there were 80 emerging adults in attendance.

The emerging adults leader stood with a microphone and welcomed everyone, and gave instructions on the barbeque (where the queue starts, vegetarian options etc).

Emerging adults got their food and socialized with each other in the courtyard and the foyer. Leaders and older emerging adults who had been in the group for several years, went between different smaller huddles, introducing themselves if necessary, asking about their weeks, and what they do for work or what they study.

At 8.15pm, the emerging adults leader again stood with a microphone and invited everyone into the main hall, where worship was about to begin. The music in the background quietened, and the emerging adults followed into the main hall, still mostly continuing their conversations.

The main hall was dark, only lit by fairy lights and colourful LEDs. There were no seats so the emerging adults gathered in lines and huddles. The worship leader stood in front of the stage with an acoustic guitar, quietly playing. Within a few minutes, the emerging adults were quiet. The worship leader played and sang, and lyrics appeared on the overhead screens.

Set List:

> *O Come to the Altar,* Elevation Worship
> *Make Room,* Elyssa Smith
> *My Testimony,* Elevation Worship
> *Phenomena,* Hillsong
> *Let Go,* Hillsong
> *Battle Belongs,* Phil Wickham

After the final song, the emerging adults leader said that people were welcome to leave if they would like to, but the auditorium would be open for thirty minutes longer, with a ping pong table, PlayStation, tuck shop and board games available too. The leader reminded the emerging adults of connect groups that will restart the following week, and to get in contact if they did not have a connect group, or would like pastoral support through the week.

Approximately 30 emerging adults left at this point. By the time the doors were closing after 30 minutes, approximately 10 emerging adults remained.

Once the emerging adults had left, the team gathered to debrief. They spoke about any issues or celebrations, and prayed for the emerging adults, and they were reminded of where to access connect group session plans. The evening finished with the team clearing up.

4

Creating Community

> 'What keeps me in church is definitely connecting with people and the relationship side; creating solid community family. Society is a mixture of old and young working together, and that is what church needs to be like.'
>
> Matthew, an emerging adult

Small Groups

Small groups, sometimes known as house / connect / midweek groups, can be helpful in engaging emerging adults. Small groups bring opportunity for discussion, debating, hearing different perspectives and experiences of others, and building community, some of which can perhaps be difficult at a Sunday service. Speaking to emerging adults, they did not seem to have a preference about whether these small groups had a mixture of ages, or were for their age group only. They recognized that whilst it was helpful to meet with people who were experiencing similar things to themselves, there was wisdom and fruit to be found in community with older generations. For many new Christians—not just emerging adults—stepping into church for the first time, they belong before they believe. Small groups are a great opportunity to grow that feeling of belonging, whilst also providing a space for discipleship.

Do you have emerging adults in your church, who do not yet attend a small group? Perhaps you could personally invite them to one.

Serving

Youth for Christ's gap year programme, The Year Out, sees a bunch of emerging adults serving in a church or Youth for Christ centre, whilst also receiving training, being mentored and discipled and experiencing community with the other volunteers. Although they mainly serve in youth work contexts, they also have opportunity to serve the wider church in toddler groups, hospitality, social action and worship.

Gap year programmes such as The Year Out provide emerging adults with opportunity to find belonging with like-minded people, ask questions, express doubts, grow in emerging adulthood, all whilst serving the local church. It is not just beneficial because groups have an extra pair of hands through a volunteer, it is more than that. The host churches invest in the emerging adults, discipling them, empowering them, whilst the volunteers feel part of something as they give to communities, groups and projects. They sense belonging through teams, and through the people they are serving. The Year Out also has a 'Homegrown' stream, in which emerging adults can choose their home church as their placement. This option can be a brilliant way to keep emerging adults in the home church and invest in them as they invest in the community.[13]

Spotting passions within the young people and emerging adults you currently have can be a great way not only to encourage serving, but also make them feel like they have a place. Many older young people take steps away from church because they feel too old for youth group, but too young for any other group. Empowering them to volunteer can help them feel like there is still a space for them. Bear in mind, however, appropriate spaces for them to volunteer in. Leading friends just a year or two younger than them does not always work, so perhaps point them in the direction of the children's groups, worship or hospitality teams, or empower them to take a lead on social media or a social action project. Try to resist subliminal gender stereotypes too; boys may like to join toddler groups and hospitality, just as girls may like to be on the PA team or set up.

One emerging adult I spoke to said that church is about serving and not just getting stuff out of it, recognizing the consumer conflict. They went on to say, '...but to know it's worth serving, I want to know that they're giving to me too. If I think it's not relevant and I'm not getting anything out of it, I'm not going to stay and serve.' Again, there is a wider conversation to be had around church being consumeristic and transactional.

Jess's Story

Jess, a student and young adults' curate, shared with me that perhaps this age group are experiencing disappointment with the church.

In Luke 24, Jesus appears to a couple of disciples on the road to Emmaus. They have had first-hand experience of Jesus' ministry, and yet now they have experienced this trauma. They say, 'This wasn't what we had hoped for' (Luke 24.21), and they do not recognize that it is in fact the resurrected Jesus walking alongside them on this road. Similarly, perhaps emerging adults are disappointed that church is not what they hoped for. They have experienced trauma—the pandemic, relationship issues, moving from home—and they are disappointed that the church is not what they hoped it would be, it perhaps is not like it was when they were in youth group, and it is not what they expected it to be as an adult, and are perhaps even disappointed in God after years of unanswered prayers. Amongst all this, they are not aware of the wonders of Jesus, or the Spirit of God that is alive in the church—both of which can be obscured by disappointment.

Jess gave the analogy that navigating emerging adult ministry can sometimes be like catching fish with your hands. Someone says, 'Emerging adults want big megachurches with hundreds of people just like them,' and so you try to catch that fish. Meanwhile, another person says 'Emerging adults feel lost in the big crowds of megachurches; they want small, authentic community,' and so you go to grab that fish instead.

When I asked Jess 'Why emerging adults?' she answered that it had always been about students for her, and that has evolved through ministry. 'I've seen students come alive in their faith, so I've thought that must be possible at any age. I've seen so many people come alive in their faith when they've become part of a community that is for them, that's rooted in Jesus. Places of belonging is what people yearn for.'

I asked Jess what has worked for her context, and what can be transferable. She answered, 'The power of home.' Many emerging adults that walk through the church doors are in a city different from the one they grew up in. They have moved for university or for work, and so to feel at home in church is significant. This can be achieved through belonging, creating community, and, practically, by having meals around the table. Jess said that relationships have been built by sharing food with the emerging adults she journeys with. 'There's power in organized spontaneity,' Jess says. 'I've had in my calendar for weeks that we're going to have a barbecue, but when I message an emerging adult with a few day's notice and personally invite them to this seemingly spontaneous barbecue we're having, they turn up.' But it is not all separate; Jess said that anyone and everyone was spontaneously invited to the barbecue, again creating this feeling of community and belonging.

The church held a summer 'Big Weekend' that all families were invited to, which Jess said helped the emerging adults to see that it is all 'joined up and not separate, they're part of a family.' Even if the emerging adults only attend the student's small group, there are opportunities to connect with the wider church as one family.

Application

- Be conscious that many emerging adults may be experiencing disappointment with the church. Journey with them, disciple them, spend some with on them and ask where they are at.
- What does belonging look like in your context? If you have two emerging adults, could you commit to having dinner with them every week? In a context with 100 emerging adults, this might not be practical. Could you instead gather a team that will weekly check in with emerging adults via text, with an invitation to a chat over coffee?
- Have faith. 'I've seen students come alive in their faith.' When have you seen emerging adults grow and bear fruit? Hold onto that as you navigate emerging adult ministry.

5

Critical Mass

Emerging adults need to be able to see that church is a space where there are people like them, at their age, facing similar age-stage issues and with whom they can build relationship. However, the idea of critical mass is a dilemma in itself, and almost brings us back to asking, 'How do we engage emerging adults?' Gaining a critical mass of emerging adults is more about attracting new emerging adults to the church, rather than engaging and keeping the ones you have got already.

Belonging

As human beings we crave belonging, and it is no different for emerging adults. Emerging adults want to fit in, both with people in similar age stages, and with older groups. This theme links with others within the booklet; it is cultivated through community and with intentionality. Through community, particularly small groups, emerging adults are invited to belong before they believe. When you think about the places and spaces where you have a sense of belonging, what was it that made you feel that way?

Ben's Story

When I was looking for a church when I moved away from home, I was looking for one that already had emerging adults, who loved their community and their family. It is really important to any emerging adult to feel like it is a home-to-home move, and my church definitely got that right. I first thought having loads of other emerging adults was important to me, and in part that is true. However, I have found it to be incredibly important to be surrounded with multi-generational families. Getting emerging adults involved in the wider church is amazing to build connections. I was not majorly looking into theology backgrounds when church-searching; I knew my comfort denominations but I really just wanted the church to surround me like a big hug and welcome me.

One of the things that engages me is consistency in contact. I think having something that is constant in a forever changing new start for an emerging adult is essential. You have just left home, left a strict education system, and potentially left a home church. It is a lot of change and uncertainty to cope with. The church can be a small and mighty thing in keeping an emerging adult sane! It sounds silly, but for me a church that looks after their emerging adults by feeding them is key!

On a Sunday, I am engaged in a preach that is both theology-based and practical for us too, something that is aimed at emerging adults. I engage best when it is stretching, but not so much that it feels like a lecture. Creative and regular social media posts help me to reengage and remember church events that are happening.

What can we learn from Ben's story?

- Many emerging adults experience change and inconsistency. Just the fact that they are emerging from youth to adulthood can be unsettling. So having a space, a family, a church that gives them some form of consistency is useful.
- Church needs to feel welcoming, like a family, a home away from home.
- Preaches aimed at emerging adults and that are practical can be engaging. There is a middle ground to be found, where a preach is challenging, stretching, has theology, but also does not feel like they are being talked at in a brain-boggling lecture.
- Being active on social media is not just engaging and attractive, but it can also serve as a helpful reminder for what is on.
- I think Ben's point about the church feeding emerging adults is one not to skim over. Frequently in the gospels we see Jesus eating with people; he invites himself to eat at Zacchaeus' house, he eats with the Pharisees, he feeds the five thousand, his last pre-resurrection moment with all the disciples is over a meal, and he eats fish on the beach post-resurrection. Furthermore, for many today, sitting around the table to eat a meal together is an important aspect of family life as it brings us together as we share a meal. Free food is both a missional and attractional model of church.

Freshers' Guide

If you are in a context near a university, freshers' week can be a great opportunity to connect in with emerging adults.

Find out when freshers' week begins. You can do this by simply typing your city, followed by 'freshers' week,' and the current year into your search engine. It is usually the second and third week of September.

You will also most likely be able to find information about a freshers' fayre, which is when organisations, charities, local businesses and societies or clubs come together to showcase their product. The university may also have events such as barbeques, colour runs, karaoke and quiz nights. You may be allowed to have a stand, give out water bottles with church branding, or give a prize for the quiz night. These methods may not feel like big wins, or like you are building relationships or successfully getting emerging adults through your doors. However, you are being intentional, being present and showing up. You are planting seeds in people's minds that the local church is alive, it is fun, it is for students. By giving away items with church branding on, you will subtly be leaving these reminders.

If there are contact details available for either the university, the Christian Union, or a freshers' president, get in touch to introduce yourself and ask what events you are able to attend. Perhaps suggest that the Christian Union visits the church one service, or offer to give a talk at one of their weekly meetings. Explain that you would both like to invite students to church, as well as be there to journey with them through the ups and downs of student life.

If you are able to attend any freshers' events, you may want to:

- Create and give out freshers' packs. These might look like paper bags including a pack of tissues, a bag of sweets, instant noodles, a highlighter and leaflets about relevant groups and services at your church.
- Wear church-branded T-shirts so that people know who you are and what you represent. This may also open up conversation.

The aim of getting in contact with a university and attending events is to build relationship with students and invite them to church. Therefore, your mission cannot end there, and you must consider what the church that you have just invited students to looks like.

The following Sunday should make the students feel that they are being welcomed home, like they could belong in this community of people.

Perhaps the talk could intentionally have references that students will understand: freshers' flu (cold-like symptoms that affect students after frequent gatherings), or pop-culture references. The talk could also be about how to hold onto faith during a new season; it could be an informal question-and-answer time with the leaders.

Finally, consider what the next 'in' is; the something that will bring emerging adults back in again, the 'carrot.' Perhaps you could:

- Organize a church-wide barbeque for a couple of weeks' time.
- Invite individual emerging adults for a coffee during the week. This will show them that you are interested in investing in them; you will have opportunity to be your authentic self, and build relationship.
- Begin a relevant sermon series: apologetics, how to keep the faith, who is Jesus? Remember the facts and figures we explored previously. Many of the new students you have invited through your doors may not be Christians, so it is important that you start at the foundations of faith, and perhaps begin to unwrap feelings emerging adults may have about the church being doubtless, inauthentic, anti-science.

6

Intentionality

One emerging adult pastor I spoke to shared that all churches have a natural bias to focus inwards and look at what they like. When it comes to suggesting a song for Sunday, they admitted to suggesting songs that they like. 'The natural bias is for churches to turn inwards. Unless you skew young, you won't have emerging adults.' Being intentional envelopes the other themes we have explored already. Community is created through intentionality, attraction is discerned and put into practice through intentionality, and critical mass is gained through intentional mission. It is important to recognize the challenges that intentionally engaging emerging adults brings, particularly for smaller churches, churches with limited staff, volunteers and finances, or for those already overburdened.

> 'The rev invited me and my friends round for dinner a few times and made an effort to invite us to all the church events. I think making an effort to include us and take an interest in our personal lives was the main reason we chose to stay, as we felt valued in the congregation.'

Taking Responsibility

Sometimes we see emerging adults as enigmatic, but church leaders must take responsibility. Youth pastors must take responsibility for raising up young people who become adults in the church. This can be done by having young people regularly sit in the main service, to debunk the idea that this is 'adult church.' When speaking from the front, instead of saying, 'When you are having conversations around the water cooler at work,' add, 'or you're in the canteen at college…' See potential in young people and emerging adults, invite them, include them, empower them.

If you have young people preparing for university, could you intentionally journey with them? The Fusion Movement sell Student Linkup Boxes, which includes resources to help students 'lay the very best foundation for your time at university and think about who you want to be, how you want to live and what you want to achieve.'[14]

You can also use the Fusion Movement website to support your young person in not only *finding* a church local to their university, but also connecting in with the leadership of the local church.

If you have emerging adults at university, could you send them a postcard that lets them know you are praying for them? Tell them that they are thought about, perhaps write them a verse, and invite them for a coffee and a catch up when they get home. This will remind emerging adults of church if they have drifted away, it will aid the feeling of belonging, and it may bring them back in whilst they are home.

Knowing and Using your Locality

Knowing and using your locality to engage emerging adults can be easier if you live in a university city. A couple of student workers I spoke to said that they create hundreds of welcome packs for freshers and they are handed out for free, they hold socials and they invite themselves to Christian Unions.

If your church is not located in a university city, you can still be where the people are. That could be a physical space, such as giving out leaflets that say 'You are welcome' and service times, speaking at college Christian Unions, or doing a social action project in places emerging adults often socialize. It could also be an online space, reaching emerging adults through YouTube, Instagram or TikTok.

Social Media Guide: Engaging Emerging Adults on Social Media

You do not need to be a graphic designer or a social media pro to create content that is engaging. Use Canva to make posts or have a look at what others are posting on social media—perhaps churches with a large emerging adult congregation, or charities such as Youth for Christ—that will have content that you can reshare.

Follow other local churches and engage with them by commenting on their posts. The comments can be as simple as, 'great stuff,' 'praise Jesus,' and 'woohoo,' or you could comment with a verse that you feel links to their post.

Use hashtags such as church, students, young adults, young adult ministry, and the name of your town or city.

Do not feel that you always have to be promoting your services. You could also post:

- A who's who of the team. Share photos on your feed, and include a short biography in the description.

- Take advantage of 'days of the year,' which can be found easily online. On National Doughnut Day, share a picture of a doughnut with a caption, 'Comment below your favourite doughnut.' It may seem like nonsense, but simple posts like these will show Instagram that you are posting regularly, which will result in you being boosted in their algorithm, thus appearing on more people's feeds.
- Share a testimony. Is there anyone in your church with a great story to share? Ask them for a photo of themselves, or find a stock photo on Unsplash or Pexels that relates to the story, and write their testimony in the caption. Remember to have the permission to share this story and write it with sensitivity.
- On World Book Day, you could share a list of the leadership team's favourite books.
- The YouVersion Bible App has verse of the day images you could reshare.

If all this sounds too difficult for whatever reason, are there any young people or emerging adults you could ask to take a lead on this?

Focus Group: Emerging Adults

If you have any emerging adults in your context, invite them to the church, a local coffee shop, or a park to discuss the following questions.

- What is your experience of church? How is the church perceived by your peers? Have you grown up through church?
- What is something, whether physical or conceptual, that you want from church?
- What topic series would you like to see?
- Would you like to serve church, and in what context? (PA, kids, social media, admin, worship, social action, emerging adults).

Focus Group: Church leadership team

Gather your church leadership team and invite any emerging adults you have to the meeting too. This shows that their voices are significant, and that there is space for them. Together, explore the following questions.

- What is your vision for the emerging adults in your locality and context? What could God be saying?

- What does it mean to be attracted to church?
- Is the application of teaching relevant to emerging adults?
- Are the worship style, groups available, and welcome attractive to emerging adults?
- What does, or could, community look like in your context?
- Are there projects and groups that emerging adults can serve?
- Are there small groups available that emerging adults can join and find belonging?
- Are there young people and emerging adults already at the church, that can get involved in acquiring critical mass?
- What is one small thing you could do to invite emerging adults to church?
- What does, or could it mean, to be intentional in your context?
- Is there someone who can drive an emerging adult ministry?
- Is there a nearby university? Can you be active on social media?

7

Conclusion

Attraction, creating community, critical mass and being intentional are all key in emerging adults. I think these themes intertwine and influence one another; emerging adults are attracted by community, authenticity, attractional models and there being a critical mass, which can begin to be achieved through intentionality.

Context, geography, budget, resources, demographics of the area and many other factors all influence the methods and the success of engaging emerging adults in church. Sometimes, we see a gap on an issue, but we get overwhelmed by its weight, so we freeze into inaction. Emerging adults' ministry can feel a lot like this. Previously, we read that a students' curate compared the ministry to catching fish with bare hands. It can feel near impossible, but take heart. You will not grow a megachurch overflowing with emerging adults overnight (and I personally suggest you need not). However, by starting small, having a vision, and being intentional, you may just begin to see some change.

Continue the Conversation

For training and resources for your church, explore fusionmovement.org.uk.[15] If you would like to read further into the conversation, I would recommend the following books:

M DeVries and S Pontier, *Sustainable Young Adult Ministry: Making it Work Making it Last* (Downers Grove, IL: IVP, 2019).

B Seversen, *Not Done Yet: Reaching and Keeping Unchurched Emerging Adults* (Downers Grove, IL: IVP, 2020).

A Stanley and S Hall, *The Seven Checkpoints for Student Leaders: Seven Principles Every Teenager Needs to Know* (New York: Howard Books, 2011).

M Swanson and Fusion Movement, *Church and Students* (Loughborough: Fusion Movement, 2021).

Notes

1 N Allan and M Allan, *The XYZ of Discipleship: Understanding and Reaching Generations Y & Z* (Malcolm Down Publishing, 2020).

2 D Fitch, *What Is the Church and Why Does It Exist?* (Herald Press, 2021).

3 Youth for Christ, 'Gen Z: Rethinking Culture,' 2016.

4 BBC Bitesize, 'Millennials, baby boomers or Gen Z: Which one are you and what does it mean?' Available at: https://www.bbc.co.uk/bitesize/articles/zf8j92p (accessed June 2022).

5 M Dinic, 'How religious are British people?' Yougov, 29 December 2020. Available at: https://yougov.co.uk/topics/lifestyle/articles-reports/2020/12/29/how-religious-are-british-people (accessed May 2022).

6 'Talking Jesus Report,' 2022, *Alpha,* the Evangelical Alliance, HOPE Together, Luis Palau Association and Kingsgate Community Church.

7 The Evangelic Alliance, 'The Young Adults Conversation.' Available at: https://www.eauk.org/what-we-do/initiatives/the-young-adults-conversation (accessed 17 October 2022).

8 B Keith, *Authentic Faith: Fresh Expressions of Church Amongst Young Adults* (Fresh Expressions, 2013).

9 D Kinnaman, *You Lost Me. Why Young Christians are Leaving the Church...and Rethinking Faith* (Grand Rapids, MI: Baker Books, 2016) pp 16, 116, 136, 193.

10 A Stanley, *Deep and Wide: Creating Churches Unchurched People Love to Attend* (Grand Rapids, MI: Zondervan, 2012) p 16.

11 J Wilson, 'Missional versus attractional: An argument the church cannot afford' *Ministry*, August 2018. Available at: https://www.ministrymagazine.org/archive/2018/08/Missional-versus-attractional-An-argument-the-church-cannot-afford (accessed July 2022).

12 B Keith, *Authentic Faith, op cit.*

13 The Year Out, Youth for Christ's gap year programme: see yfc.co.uk/theyearout (accessed 17 October 2022).

14 Fusion Student Linkup Box: see https://www.fusionmovement.org/box (accessed 17 October 2022).

15 Fusion (homepage), available at: https://fusionmovement.org (accessed 17 October 2022).